For information contact:
grisel.companioni@gmail.com
Written by Grisel Companioni and Illustrated by R.M Danushka Sandaruwan
ISBN: 9798477310449 (paperback)
Printed in the United States of America

I found an advertisement online about a farm in upstate New York that takes care of senior dogs.

There is a swimming area and plenty of dog houses.

I quickly called Buddy over to where I was sitting. I caressed his head and neck.

"Hi, Buddy, I have something to show you."
I turned my laptop towards him.
“Buddy, look at this,” I said to him, and he settled next to me.
I clicked on a video I found on the farm's website and showed it to him.

**He was barking when he saw the dogs and other animals in the video. Seeing him happy while watching, I finally made up my mind. I decided to sign him up for a temporary stay at the farm.**

I asked my friend Zelmy if she can take the four-hour drive with Buddy and me to the farm. The whole ride, I was really sad that I was going to be leaving Buddy there. He was in the back seat, enjoying the view on the way to the farm.

**As we got closer to the farm, we first saw the barn and a big house.**

When Zelmy, Buddy,
and I got out of the
car and walked a
little bit, we saw
many dogs, horses,
chickens, and alpacas.
Buddy was happy
to see all the animals.

The caretaker of
the farm greeted us,
and he took hold
of Buddy's leash.

I kneeled to give Buddy a big hug and kiss. I told him to be a good boy and that I will return for him. Zelmy also said goodbye. We watched as he walked Buddy onto the property. All the animals were curious as to who Buddy was. Buddy was wagging his tails as he walked with the caretaker.

This was the first time that I was going to be far away from Buddy, but I knew he would very much enjoy being around so many other dogs. I would call the caretakers at the farm every so often to ask how Buddy was doing.

They would inform me that Buddy was doing very good and made so many new friends. He particularly spends a lot of time playing with a dog named David. David's dog house was located about a mile from Buddy's dog house.
The caretaker said Buddy walks that mile every morning to visit David.

David and Buddy became best friends in a short period of time. The day came for me to pick up Buddy and take him home. I was so excited to see him. As I waited for him outside, I saw the caretaker walking Buddy, and he had almost 30 dogs behind him walking as well. It was like they knew Buddy was going home, and they wanted to say goodbye.

When Buddy saw me, he was so happy that he jumped up with excitement and kept giving me kisses. He was making noises as if he was trying to speak to me. I gave him a big hug and said Buddy; we are going home now. In the car on the drive home, I told him how much I missed him and how happy I was to have him come home.

www.ingramcontent.com/pod-product-compliance
Lightning Source LLC
LaVergne TN
LVHW071113160826
845679LV00004B/1066

*9798477310449*